On Dreams and Reality

Elvira Salyahetdinova

BookLeaf Publishing

Presentation by *BookLeaf Publishing*

Web: www.bookleafpub.com

E-mail: info@bookleafpub.com

ISBN : 9789357699273

First edition 2022

DEDICATION

To my sisters, to my mother.

For their love is like no other

The Baby Asked

What is Life? - The baby asked.
I wish I knew - The mother wondered too.

But you brought me here with you.
You surely know a thing or two?

I will tell you this as I care for you:

Life is music and you will dance to it.
Life is long if you hear its endless song.
Life is space and you will find your pace.
Life is magic if you do not think it is tragic.
Life is a mystery and you will see it in your
history.
Life is a fairy poem if you feel inspired by its
every column.

The Flower and Me

Do not just sit and stare at me,
The world awaits for you to be!

You can stay and contemplate,
But your life is here to change!

You tell me I don't move
I disagree - the flow is also part of me

I bloom, I weather and I am free
As I have also chosen to be me

So be like a flower, be my guest
Take a petal and leave the rest

As a single part reveals
The scent, the colour and the wills

Go on, bloom, just feel free
Find your meadow - shine endlessly!

To my Elder Sister

They introduced you as my sister.

I believed them,
maybe for a year,
maybe just for two…

But they forgot to
mention that I will find
my true friend in you!

To my Younger Sister

You told me you were dreaming…
You said you were believing…
I did not know what you were feeling…

At the end I realised -
You became a miracle by believing in your inner being!

Innocent Thoughts

What is a dream and what is reality?
Maybe the answer is high above the gravity?

What is a parent and what is a child?
Maybe they both know how to be wild?

What is freedom and what is a sleigh?
Maybe they show us the meaning of play?

What is falling and what is a slope?
Maybe they measure our endless hope?

What is purple and what is white?
Maybe they reveal our inner light?

The Soul of the Building

The signage was hanging:
"To be demolished at last"

The memories we built
Are to be ruined so fast?

The soul of the building
Made foundation for us

The sill of the entry
Counted days which we passed

The torch in the house
Showed the love between us

The stair in the corner
Measured with steps the feelings in us

The door of the attic
Shielded from rumours, from mass

The window on the roof
Displayed worlds on a cloudy atlas

The gate of the basement
Stored aims we did not surpass

The tree in the garden
Inspired growth of roots within us

The porch, so light, so vast
"Welcome", but it did not last

This precious memory of us
Collapsed to a stone from the past

My Colour Blue

What a pleasure!
I just found my treasure!
There are no units to measure,
But believe me - it is huge and I found it at my leisure

It happened when I spent a week or two, just with me and my colour blue
The first day the dark hue wanted me to feel it too

I stared and I will tell you that - the inner picture did not make me glad
It was gloomy, I was sad, I did not know I was feeling bad

Yes it is true, I had an ache or two. But surely everyone has them too
A small wound in the inner part, by the chest or by the heart

"Why should I bother and spend the time with you my ache, when I only want a break?"

But my colour made me stay and there I was -
silent, still and staring through all the feelings
dressed in navy hue

Up till then I thought I knew what I felt and
what was true

But they showed me wisdom, showed me
strength, showed me what sad feelings really
meant

The next day the colour changed to neon blue
"What a vibrant shade are you!"

The colour looked at me and smiled
"For sure you know the reason why.
You felt the feeling, it made you new
And now you have this hue in you!"

At the end, all filled with pleasure - I was
standing still, admiring my treasure
And I assure you all - this hue made such a
vibrant picture of my soul!

Inner Twilight

Twinkle, twinkle my dear friend
Where is your passion, where is your flame?

It is not me who has the blame
Within resides a stranger with no name
Without a structure, without a frame
Comes and goes, I just cannot explain
Hide and seek is his famous game

You might proclaim
"This is the hunchback of Notre Dame!"

No my dearest of my friends
It is far from any fairy tale
It does not ask for any fame
It is silent, it is violent

Without a notice, without a plane
Flies directly in my vein
It takes my faith, it causes pain
Leaves empty where I stored my aim

But I am sure my dear friend,
You can end this misery, this drain
Do not waste your days in vain
You can end this twilight of your brain

Find what is true and what is plain
Find your passion, find your flame
Just allow faith to enter in your vein

My Sister's Past

My dear sister, where is home?
You were not here when I was born
What is this place you are coming from?

In this place you called your own

Did you have a palace with a crystal dome?
Did you have your very own unicorn?
Did you fly from dusk till dawn?
Did the sky have endless sunshine drown?
Did you touch the rainbows you were shown?
Did you have a golden harp to play along?
Maybe angels sang a tender song?

When the time came for you to join

Did you know the way your eyes would be
drawn - the colour and the form?
Did they say what makes the world so wrong?
Did they tell you to have faith and to be strong?
Did you know what the future will bring on?
Did they send you with an Evensong?
Maybe all was crystal clear my dear?

My sister never answered that…
I knew she had her secret past

To Learn to Say Goodbye

Within the woods
Within the wooden boxes

A lesson started
Among the foxes

"To learn to say goodbye"

The teacher said
With a cunning smile

"To learn to say goodbye?
Why would I?"

A tiny voice filled the air
A tiny fox was sitting on a chair

"I spent the time to introduce me
And now I will let somebody lose me?"

"You said hello, you had a blast,
The time has come for it to pass

When you truly care for one another
You would not want to hunt the other

You would want to set him free
You would choose to let him be

You would wish him all the best
You would put an end, give him rest

You would find you passed the test
You would find you learned the best

When something would not last
You simply store it in your past"

A Scan for Souvenir

The doctors said:
"Please come in"

They would only scan
My being from within

There I was, laying on the bed
Silent, ready for them to check

Biopsy of my feelings
Autopsy of my brain

A needle in my heart
Anaesthesia for the pain

Their search was not in vain
They found a substance in my vein

"We took a sample, we did the test
It reveals you have the courage,
you have the zest"

At the end they gave a scan
Something like a souvenir

To remind me what I can

When I forget about the fear

The Little Boy

The sparkle, the music, the toy
The festive season and the festive joy
Such a lovely Christmas to enjoy

Not until we found a homeless boy…
“Poverty is a virtue”
Would have said Tolstoy

He was starving, he was freezing
Feeling hopeless and not believing
In the “good” people who are always leaving

We could close our eyes, refuse to see the pain, the misery
But we saw his love, his victory and that was the greatest mystery

Someone said:
“This is what he chose his life to be.
We should stay away from this agony”

I strongly disagree!
Even without a home,
he still belonged to me

We gave him food, I gave the toy

He gave us hope, he gave us joy
What luck to find this lovely boy!

The Cherub's Waving Hand

You were sitting on the wooden stand
A statue of a cherub with a waving hand

Was I dreaming, was it real
When you started to appeal

You said:
"Believe in me!

This Christmas Eve arrived at last
To bring magic from the holly past"

You said you would explain to me
What our eyes could not see

You said the flight would not take us long
To where the ethereal and divine belong

"How do we enter this spiritual realm?"
"By not having any thoughts of harm"

An endless bliss was
our childlike game

You came and planted in my brain
The seed of faith and eternal flame

And now I know the riddle
From my angel's game:

"Why does a cherub wave a hand?
To plant love in a barren land"

February 14

The day of love
The day to be
To give my joy selflessly

The friend I want
The chance to meet
To show and share our bliss

The day has gone
The day was spent all alone
To contemplate on and on

The night has come
The truth was there
To face myself and take self care

The task was clear
The love I give
To be for all and for me

The joy I have
The wings to spread
To fly solo is also artistry

The rose I want
The rose in me

To let it bloom beautifully

The friend I want
The friend is me
To love myself endlessly

Burning Bridges

Thought we were headed to eternity
Thought you and me - will forever be

You were standing on the shore
You did not come with me

I crossed the muddy river
I crossed and I was dry and free

There was fire
There was, in me

To burn the bridges
To find paradise, in me

Dear Little Bumblebee

Dear little bumblebee
Do you still remember me
We met under the cherry tree?

It was sunny, I was a child
I got you in my cup for tea
Invited you to play with me

You were buzzing
"You are excited to play with me!"
But you wanted me to set you free

I never knew my bumblebee
What harm you could cause to me
What a scary creature you could be

Do you remember little bumblebee
When you stung your poison into me
And you took the breath out of me?

I was swollen, I was red
"I am too young to be dead"
Would have said the humble me

There were prayers, there was hope
The doctor stung with his metal wasp

"She will still continue to breathe"

I forgive you my little bee
You did not know I had an allergy
You were only scared of me

I asked:
"Where is my friend?
Where is my little bumblebee?"

They said:
"You should find another friend
The one you had thinks you are the enemy"

Now I understand my little friend
You did not want to stop my breath
You were only scared to death

The Faberge

A day spent in the gallery
A day to flee, feel free

A day spent in solitary
A day to spend with me

Sitting in the canteen
Drinking cup of tea

A foreign woman next to me
Approached and spoke to me

“Did you see the exhibition,
Belle Amie?"

"An exhibition?
Was there one to see?"

The exhibition was on Fabergé
The eggs he made for royalty

I left my cup of tea
I run to the entrance of the gallery

“Sold out till May”
The woman said honestly

I could not see the bejewelled artistry
But one thing I could clearly see

There were so many strangers
With interests like me!

Mirror on the Wall

Mirror, mirror on the wall
Will I ever wise up and grow?

Mirror, mirror on the wall
Should I share my love and joy?

Mirror, mirror on the wall
Should I worry about the bully, the foe?

Mirror, mirror on the wall
I can see your cracks, you are not whole

Mirror, mirror on the wall
Are these cracks also in my soul?

Mirror, mirror on the wall
I took your frame, I changed your glass

Mirror, mirror on the wall
Your reflection is my wise compass

Weather Forecast

"Stay at home
It is a must

The hurricane
Will come to pass!"

An empty room
There I was

"This is a challenge
From my past!"

An open book
A memoir

I looked in it
I found a scar

I healed my soul
Some time ago

A ruin was there
Did not want to go

The wind just passed
It freed my past

I spent the time
I wrote forecast:

“After ruins
You will have contrast

After sorrows
You will have a blast!”

Prima Ballerina

Your dream did not faint
Of the prima who was a friend

Was it yesterday when you
Woke up and danced?

The music, the lights, the show
The beauty you felt in your soul

"You are not the best"
This was a contest!

Now you had to learn
To express your best

The end of the beginning
The beginning of the end

Maybe years have passed
Maybe you felt crushed

The dream you had
The dream was gone

Crossed the world so vast
Learned the mastery at last

You finally came home
Your dream was to perform

"What a talent!
Not a single flaw!"

The truth as white as snow
You knew before the show

That little girl they saw
Had a ballerina in her soul!

The Promise

Dear little me
Have you ever imagined
What life would be?

Almost thirty years
On this Earth
You and me

We saw some joy
We saw some tragic
But we still believe in magic

Dear little me, please promise me
To never forget to live the rest
With the highest hope you can ever get!

www.ingramcontent.com/pod-product-compliance
Lightning Source LLC
Chambersburg PA
CBHW051748130826
49812CB00033B/1057
9789357699273